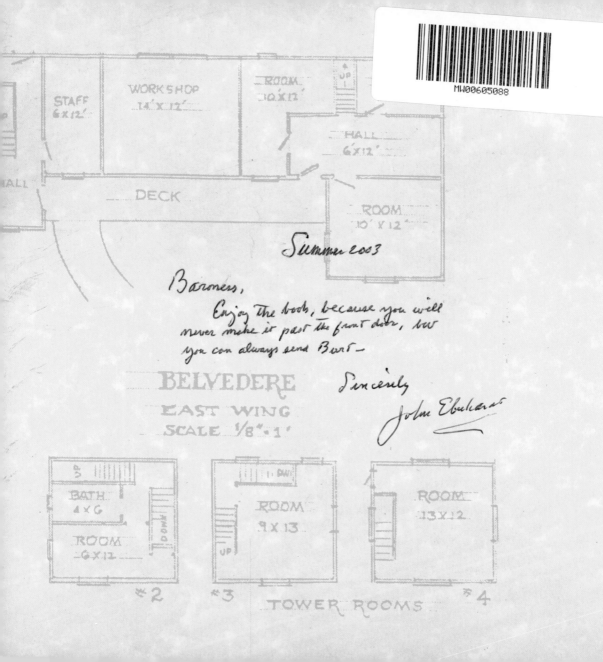

STAFF
6'X12'

WORKSHOP
14'X12'

ROOM
10'X12'

UP

HALL

HALL
6'X12'

DECK

ROOM
10'X12'

Summer 2003

Baroness,

Enjoy the book, because you will never make it past the front door, but you can always send Bart —

Sincerely

John Eberhardt

BELVEDERE
EAST WING
SCALE 1/8"=1'

BATH
4X6

ROOM
6'X12'

UP

DOWN

#2

ROOM
9X13

DW

UP

#3

ROOM
13X12

#4

TOWER ROOMS

THE BELVEDERE

Book design by Mark Guillory
Edited by Adrian Milton
Photographs copyright © 1999, Grant Lukenbill

First Edition, 2000

ACKNOWLEDGEMENTS

We owe a great debt of thanks and gratitude to John Eberdardt, owner of the Belvedere, for his loyal support and unwavering patience with the process of bringing this book to print over the past six years. We also thank his lifelong friend Joe Fiorentino as well as the many guests and friends who graciously indulged our research efforts, numerous questions, and photographic equipment—at times in the midst of their personal vacations.

We thank Patrick Arena for writing the song "Belvedere," and David Rogers for his early photographic contributions as well as his fine portraits of John Eberhardt.

We also express our sincere appreciation and gratitude to the people of the Damron Company for believing in this work—especially the hardworking art director, Mark Guillory, who kept his eyes on everything including important little details that we surely would have missed without his dedication.

Grant Lukenbill Adrian Milton February 8, 2000.

$\mathscr{C}$ONTENTS

About Belvedere

Upon arriving at Belvedere, you are welcomed onto the grounds through a set of large wrought iron gates. Just inside the entranceway, the face of a classical Greek goddess gently spews water from its mouth into a fountain. Behind it, the wall is covered with mirrors and overlaid with slender pilasters and ornate wooden carvings of fruit and flowers. Upon approaching the house, a door covered with lacy iron filigree beckons the visitor to investigate what mystery hides behind it. As the walkway continues, a realization begins to unfold—that the vision of Belvedere is one of endless delight and creativity. The entire property reveals itself to be a magical place accented by unexpected niches, intriguing corridors, and exotic juxtapositions that excite the senses.

Unfortunately, there is no more space to expand the buildings or courtyards of this dreamlike palazzo. Instead, a continual elaboration on the present elements continues this artistic endeavor. A new balustrade around the roof, castings for the tops of doors, windows, and crown moldings are among the ongoing projects. And of course, there are constant repairs as the ravages of the winter winds and sea air take a heavy toll on this, the grandest of all properties on Fire Island.

Over fifty other houses have been built in the style of Belvedere on Fire Island, but very few remain intact in their original state. Over the years they have been sold and resold, with the new owners adding second stories and wings and often altering the facades. However, some of the houses within walking distance of Belvedere still maintain their builders' original designs. Their names have a timeless connection to the dream of Belvedere that inspired them: Bottom of the Garden, Roman Holiday, Hansel and Gretel, Rabbit Hill, and Victoria and Albert. All of these structures continue to express the elegant, neoclassical touch that is their hallmark.

Great effort and ingenuity were expended in the building of Belvedere. Lumber and other supplies were laboriously hauled from the main dock of Cherry Grove. Architectural artifacts from old buildings were used to create an unusual rendition of a Palladian villa. The structure and the design were improvised during construction. Often, a fragment suggested an entire room.

The first piece of property built in the style of Belvedere, and to hold that name, was located on Maryland Walk, not far from the Great South Bay. Later the name was transferred to the great guest house on the bay and the original house was renamed the House of Orange.

During the early years of construction only handsaws were used, as there was no electricity. All illumination was provided by oil lamps, candles, chandeliers, or gas light fueled by propane tanks. The globes on the gas lights had to be periodically changed. Those who lived on Fire Island in this period remember the twinkling gas lighting and its romantic atmosphere. A dinner party at Belvedere would be illuminated by hundreds of candles and gas wall sconces. At night, it was very dark outside as there was no outdoor lighting. Those out walking at night had to carry a flashlight in order to find their way around the island.

Furniture and building supplies, as well as all food, came to the dock and were loaded onto wagons. A rented barge was used to move things from the mainland. Sometimes the barge would get stuck in the shallow waters of the bay about fifty feet from the house, and furniture would have to be carried through the water. The water was rarely more than eighteen inches deep, and planks and sawhorses were set up to haul everything ashore. The manner in which Belvedere was constructed and its placement at the marshy edge of the bay invokes comparison with Venice. Even the mayor of Venice once sent a flag as a gift along with a book on Venetian architectural elements, for inclusion among Belvedere's many treasures. Today, the chief flag of Belvedere is the flag of St. Mark's of Venice. But, in keeping with a long tradition among the residents of Fire Island, Belvedere also flies the American flag and the rainbow flag.

Whatever parts of Belvedere that were not built with new material were assembled from bits and pieces of architectural fragments taken from old mansions in Newport, the North Shore of Long Island, and the estate country of New Jersey. As modernism triumphed and large staffs of servants became too costly, many of the great houses from the turn of the century were wantonly destroyed by the wrecker's ball. A constant search was made for architectural and artistic elements to incorporate into this fantasy house. This relentless pursuit has resulted in the acquisition of some stunning fragments. Belvedere features massive oak doors rescued from "Penn-Craig" in Newport, seven-foot-high mahogany doors that once hung in the Harry Sinclair house on Long Island's North

Shore, and mantelpieces, door frames, and windows from a North Shore house that belonged to the Astors.

Invitations to the many parties held at Belvedere have always been among the most coveted of the Fire Island season. Like most Cherry Grove parties of yore, these events had a theme. Invitations were sent to a house and the owner of the house would bring an entourage of costumed guests. Everyone was expected to dress in the style of the party's theme. One year it might be an eighteenth-century court gala, an MGM Evening of the Stars, a Mid-Summer's Eve diversion, or a revel fashioned around an ancient Roman banqueting hall. Great beauties with well-developed bodies wore little silk nothings, while other guests donned togas or came as plenipotentiaries from exotic faraway places. Some guests arrived by barges fitted  out to look like swans, pulled through the water by muscular men dressed as janissaries.

Since those days, the physical expansion of Belvedere has long stopped, and development in Cherry Grove reached its final stage in the late 1970s. At that time, most of the island was made part of a national seashore and no more building beyond the borders of that time have been permitted. But the spirit of the land, and the dream of the man behind the vision that is known worldwide as Belvedere, lives on.

THE MAN BEHIND THE DREAM

As a child, John Eberhardt was always sketching and painting. During the late forties he did scenic painting for ABC and CBS. In 1947 he visited Europe and bought many antiques. Because of the chaos in Europe in the aftermath of World War II, antique furniture and objets d'art were relatively inexpensive. When he returned to America, his stateroom was piled high with old chairs, paintings, bronzes, and bric-a-brac.

The experience of working as a set designer and scenic artist taught John Eberhardt much about creating dramatic effects. He transferred these talents to Belvedere and created murals and easel paintings to embellish his architectural creations. Much of the work was done in Florida during the winter at his house in Palm Beach, the Villa Fontana, and then transported to Fire Island.

John Eberhardt first visited Fire Island in the spring of 1956. He was so impressed with Cherry Grove that he returned the next weekend, bought a building lot, and immediately began building a house. Joe Fiorentino, his partner and co-host of Belvedere for many years, helped him with much of the work, hauling supplies and lumber from the dock.

Over the years a change has occurred in John Eberhardt's artistic palette. His older palette consisted of gray, umber, mossy green, and shades of purple and lavender. His work in the new West Wing is brighter, with more pistachios and cerises, rather in the style of Austrian High Baroque. Claude Lorraine, Vernet, and Hubert Robert are among his chief influences. The neoclassical ethos still inspires him and he is happy to be continuing a long and venerable tradition. He styles himself a decorative artist who paints walls, ceilings, furniture, columns, and much more to create an ambiance for elegant living. However, many of his paintings stand alone as superb artistic achievements.

John is known for his dry wit and love of life. He is always the gracious host and works very hard to keep his vision alive. Although there is a mock-theatrical quality to Belvedere, derived from its quality of pastiche, improvisation, and camp, it ultimately stands as a significant creation and grand tribute to its creator as well as a regal embellishment to Fire Island.

In a quiet corner of Belvedere, there is a small baroque chapel, which was consecrated by a visiting Roman Catholic bishop. When asked why, Eberhardt replied, "Every great house in Italy has a chapel and so it only seemed fitting to have one here." He added that when he dies he wants his ashes to be sealed in an urn and then placed inside the Belvedere's chapel.

EXTERIORS

Imparting an air of royal arrival, the grand gate is flanked by statues of seated lions that once graced the Rodman Wannamaker residence. Just beyond, in a fountain guarded by caryatids and reflected by mirrored archways, water gently gurgles into a Roman-style basin.

An inviting neoclassical pool house provides a cool place to escape the summer sun.

Branches of weeping willows lazily dangle over the sheltered hot tub area. A statue of Neptune, god of the sea, suggests an hour or two of watery relaxation.

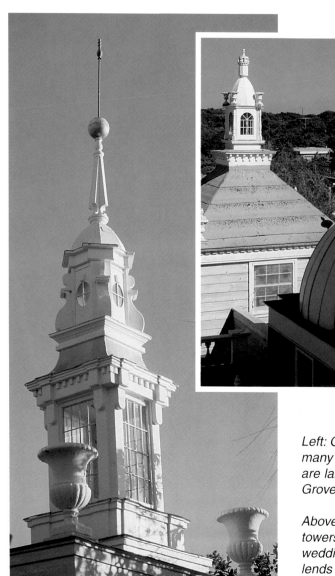

Left: One of Belvedere's many baroque towers that are landmarks on the Cherry Grove skyline.

Above: The domes and towers of Belvedere have a wedding-cake quality that lends an air of delightful fantasy to Cherry Grove.

This baroque tower with its ornate cupola sporting a lantern is a beacon at night to Fire Island revelers.

Right: A vine-covered trellis casts cooling shadows over the entry courtyard.

Above Left: The entry doors came from a Victorian Gothic house in Newport. The two lanterns flanking it once hung on the gates of the Vanderbilt estate in Oakdale, Long Island.

Below Right: An Eberhardt mural on the ceiling above the entry doors welcomes each new visitor.

The entry double doors are an imposing sentry hiding the wonders beyond.
Visitors are asked to brush their feet off so as not to track island sand inside.

Sunlight casts dappled patterns on two caryatids who beckon visitors to explore Belvedere's shady walkways.

Apollo Belvedere, presiding deity of the house, towers over the guest pool. This replica of the Vatican statue epitomizes all the ideals of Eberhardt's vision.

A sun-dappled lion serves as a sentinel between two courtyards. The arched passageway frames the view beyond like a piece of art.

A lead statue of a muse, painted white, presides over the deck leading to the bay. It came from an old music hall in New Jersey which was torn down.

11

A bust of the Emperor Hadrian greets visitors as they enter Belvedere's inner sanctum.

Rome's greatest emperor, Hadrian presided over the ancient world with wisdom and style. He created the Villa Adriana, the largest palace ever built, which is now a vast ruin outside of Tivoli, Italy.

A velvety-red bloom soaks up the afternoon sun cast on the weathered edge of a fountain.

Afternoon light dances through a maze of wisteria branches dangling seed pods over the walkway to Belvedere's main reception foyer.

Water trickles over the lip of a fountain as the early morning sun catches its glistening drops.

Left: Rusting planters with their finish eaten away by the salty sea air await a fresh coat of paint. Right: A post, embellished with a rosette, supports an orb finial.

17

INTERIORS

Every room in Belvedere projects a different mood. The ambiance ranges from the formal elegance of the Grand Salon and the public rooms to the intimacy of the suites. The guests can imagine themselves in the residence of a doge, nobleman, queen, gigolo, or any number of characters out of the pages of history. The many unique and interesting pieces of furniture, statuary, bibelots, paintings, carvings, and artistic oddities to be found on the premises excite the imagination and contribute to the overall fantasy effect.

Preceding Page: The Grand Salon of
the private quarters is a lavish study
in baroque elegance.

Above Left: The multi-textured
surfaces combine to create an air of
subdued elegance.

Above Right: A view of the elegant
seating area from above.
Left: A large eighteenth-century
mirror above the Louis XV mantel.

An accumulation of objets d'art sit astride the grand, which has been the locale of many a songfest at cocktail hour. Marie Antoinette's cradle has become a planter for bamboo.

Above: This bust of a handsome Greek god rests serenely on its pedestal.

Right: Classical busts line an arched passageway.

Opposite Page: An Oriental runner stretches along a passageway lined with planters and hanging baskets.

A warm glow from the wall sconces illuminates the Rococo headboard fit for the finest of gentlemen.

The mirror reflected in the mirror creates a setting that would please even the vainest of creatures.

The urns depicted in the artwork on the walls are a hallmark of the decorative elements of Belvedere.

An open door of a Louis XIII chamber beckons the visitor to enter a suite filled with all the possibilities of mystery and enchantment.

The striped wallpaper and spindled white headboard in this guest room are reminiscent of the Brighton Pavilion.

This Garden Room is blazoned in blue french wallpaper and loaded with antiques. It is among Belvedere's most requested guest quarters.

The murals, prints, paintings, antique mirrors, and elaborate headboards in each guest room add to the sense of luxury and wry elegance that many guests regard as quintessential Belvedere fun.

A painting of Venice by Eberhardt decorates this elaborate eighteenth-century headboard in the Doge's Suite.

The passageway leading to the private chapel, which has been duly sanctified by the proper ecclesiastical authorities, is strewn with crisp blossoms and greenery.

The pilastered doorway of the chapel invites one in for a quiet moment of meditation. Elegant fittings grace the altar.

*Left: Stella Maris, or Our Lady of the Sea, has a special niche in the chapel.
Above Right: This arched spandrel graces one wall. It encases a colorful,
fresco-like mural based on an early Christian catacomb wall painting. Right: The
layering of objects, such as this candlestick played against the elaborate spoked
window, provides a constant realignment of one's point of view.*

This antique Spanish crucifix was originally used in a monastery. It was purchased by Eberhardt at an auction in Newport.

A pierced teakwood chair
is an exotic example of skilled
Chinese furniture making.

An Oriental porcelain rests atop a carved Indian rosewood tambour.

A French nineteenth-century bronze statue shows a determined hero delivering the final thrust to a monster who has threatened a damsel.

Opposite Page: A statue replica depicting one of the daughters of King Louis XV of France adorns the Grand Salon from high above.

A quiet Raj-style seating ensemble in a simple room with a private view of a peaceful garden provides the perfect, comptemplative spot for gathering ones cares and thoughts.

Above: Miniature obelisks, a model of a galleon, and a pile of old books lend the rooms of Belvedere the atmosphere of a connoisseur's lair.

Right: Fine embroidery decorates the border of this shimmering silk canopy.

ARTIST'S CANVAS

One of the most distinctive
features of Belvedere is the
many fine paintings, murals,
and painted surfaces executed
by John Eberhardt. The
influence of Hubert Robert,
Claude Lorraine, the
Surrealists, and Eugene
Berman can all be detected in
his work. However, he brings
all of these elements together
in a unique manner. His
flights of fantasy center
around the ancient world and
always reflect a contemplative
and philosophical perspective.

A detail of the ceiling mural in the Grand Salon which depicts Prometheus stealing fire from the gods.

The interior of the great central dome of Belvedere is punctuated with faux portholes, ornate cartouches, and garlands.

An arched entry, surrounded by a wall covered in faux finishes, beckons one towards the registration desk.

A pair of maritime murals flank the hot tub area.

Above: A sea-green cartouche frames this Arcadian scene of an obelisk marking the entrance to an ancient port.

Right: Detail of mural. The galleons seen in these murals reflect the nautical theme found throughout much of the artwork at Belvedere.

A faux terra-cotta urn with cupids forms an ironic counterpoint to a trompe-l'oeil painting of a seashell and decorative swag.

Wood floors, painted in the trompe l'oeil style to resemble the finest marble, continue an Italian decorative tradition.

Right: A painted sunburst on the floor creates a focal point for the Grand Salon.

Above Detail: The faux marble floor painting creates a strong counterpoint to the brass floor compass ornament.

An ornate Rococo rosette draws the visitor's eye to the ceiling.

Faux finishes, along with elaborate decorative detail on the finely crafted woodwork, all work together to create a sensuous kaleidoscope of textures throughout Belvedere.

BELVEDERE

I see the blue sky
I breathe the salt air
I lie in the shade
and I dream
Belvedere

I wander the world
yearning to hear
the musical tide
I recall
Belvedere

Belvedere heal me
shield me from harm
feel the sea cast
her midsummer's
charm

I'm journeying home
to the sand & the sea
the sunlight is clear

I am near
Belvedere

Belvedere

Music and lyrics by
Patrick Arena © 2000

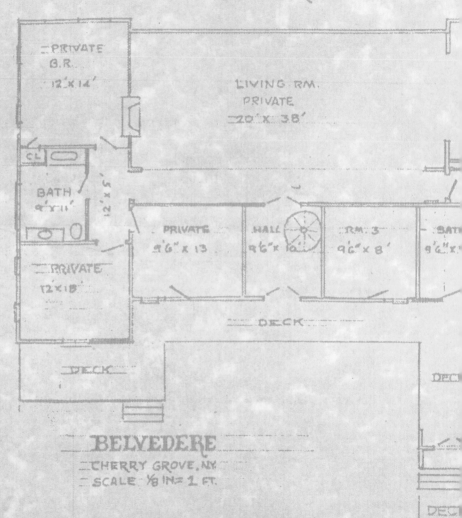

GREAT SOUTH BAY

DECK

PRIVATE
B.R.
12' x 14'

LIVING RM.
PRIVATE
20' x 38'

CL

BATH
9' x 11'

12' x 5'

PRIVATE
9'6" x 13

HALL
9'6" x 10

RM. 3
9'6" x 8'

BATH
9'6" x 1

PRIVATE
12' x 18'

DECK

DECK

DECK

DECK

BELVEDERE

CHERRY GROVE, N.Y.

SCALE: 1/8 IN = 1 FT.